A Mark Dahle Portfolio

Amanda Gets A Surprise

(#3 in the series Amanda Wanted A Miracle)

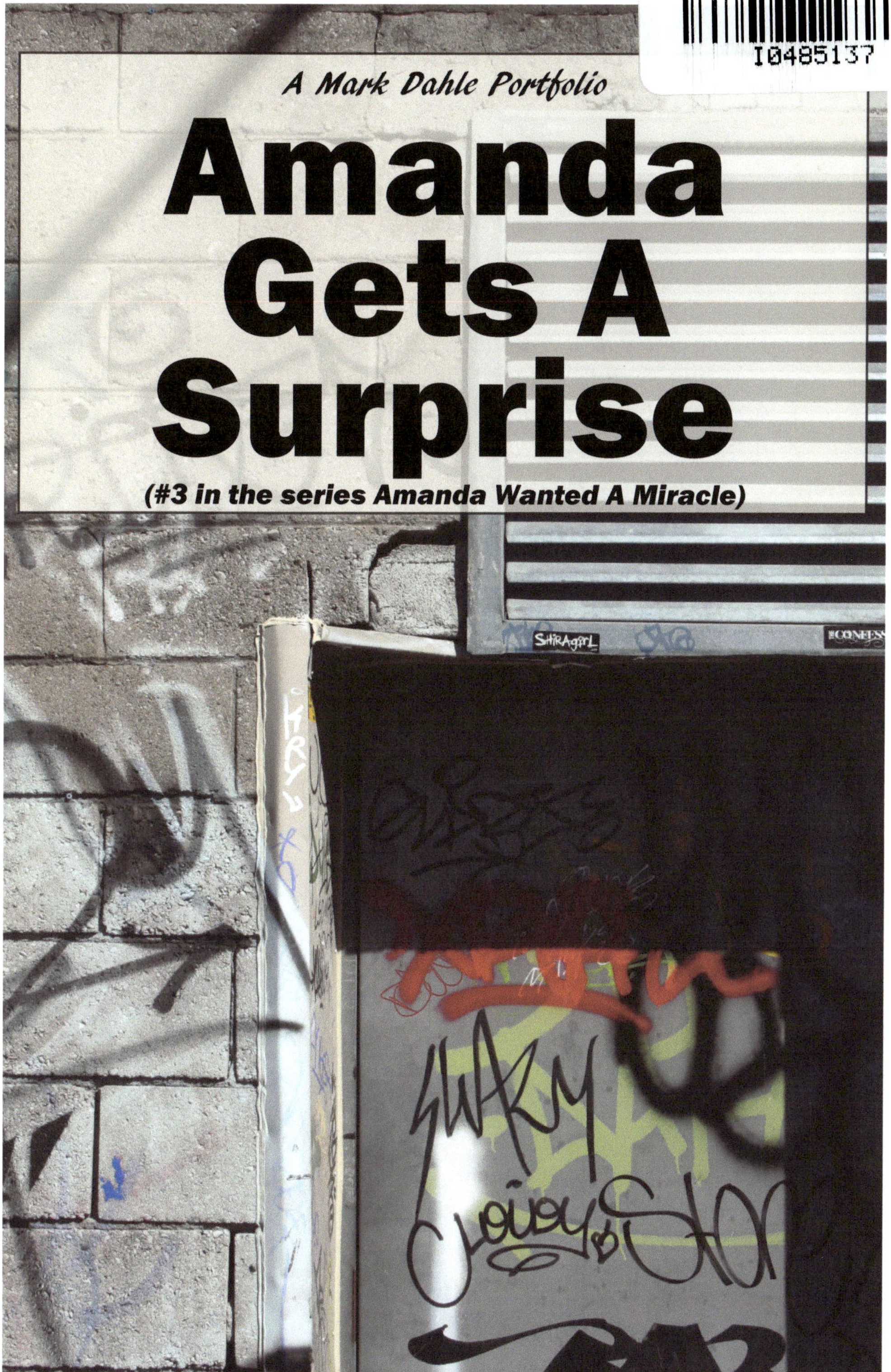

This is the third story in the series *Amanda Wanted A Miracle*. The books in this series:

1. *Amanda Gets A Pumpkin*
2. *Amanda Gets A Watermelon*
3. *Amanda Gets A Surprise*
4. *Amanda Gets A Neighbor*
5. *Amanda Gets A Miracle*

~ ~ ~

Mark Dahle Portfolios can be read in a few minutes and enjoyed for a lifetime.

Unlike many picture books, the text in this book is not related to the art. This might seem weird at first. One thing that makes it better is to order more portfolios until you get used to it. Fortunately, space is provided on the pages for you to draw your own pictures if you like.

This portfolio includes a beautiful 36 x 24 inch painting (at the right), twenty-four great photos from Toronto, and a story about Amanda, who wanted a miracle.

Photographs in this book are available in limited editions. See http://www.MarkDahle.com for more information and for previews of upcoming portfolios.

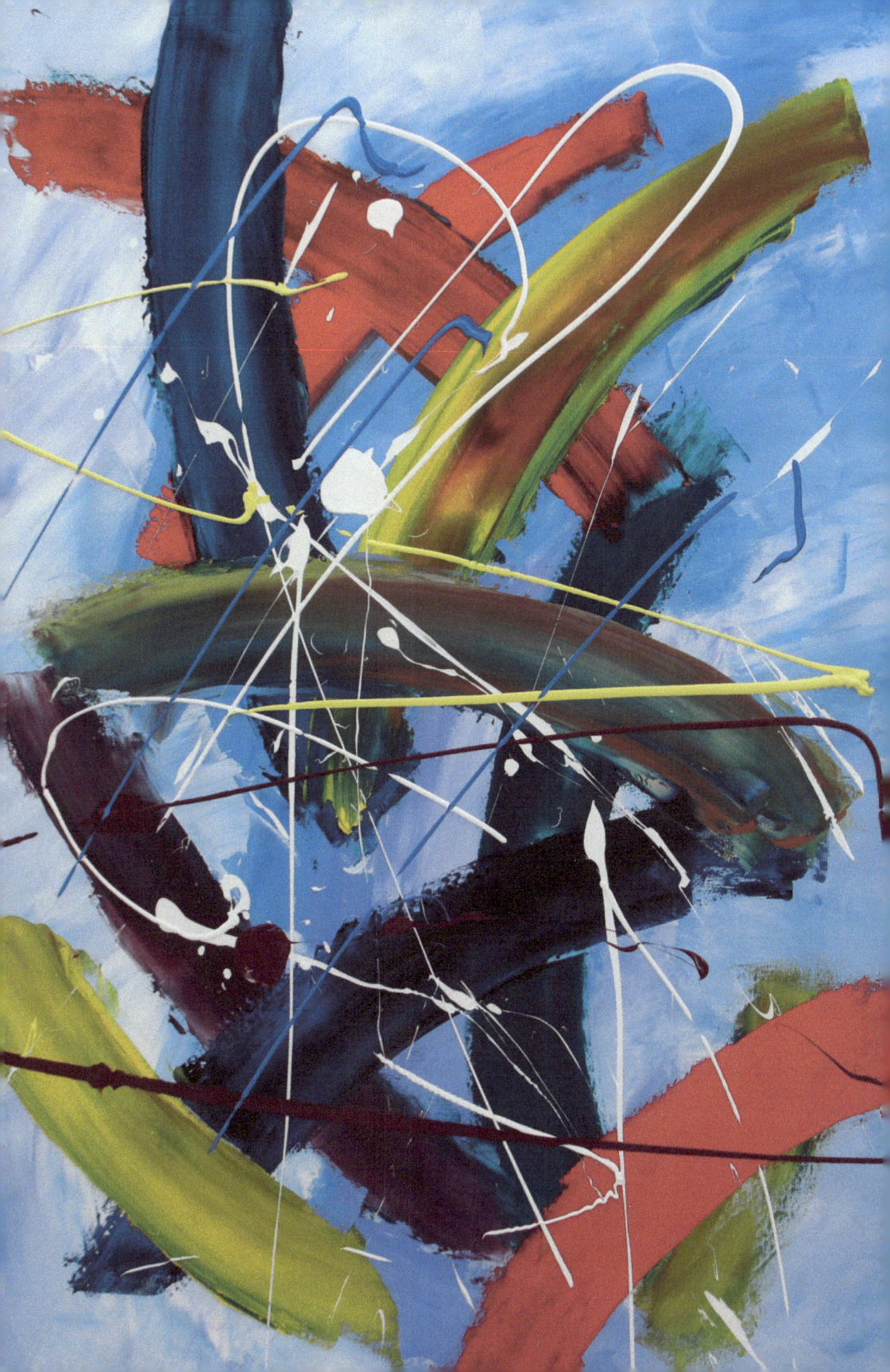

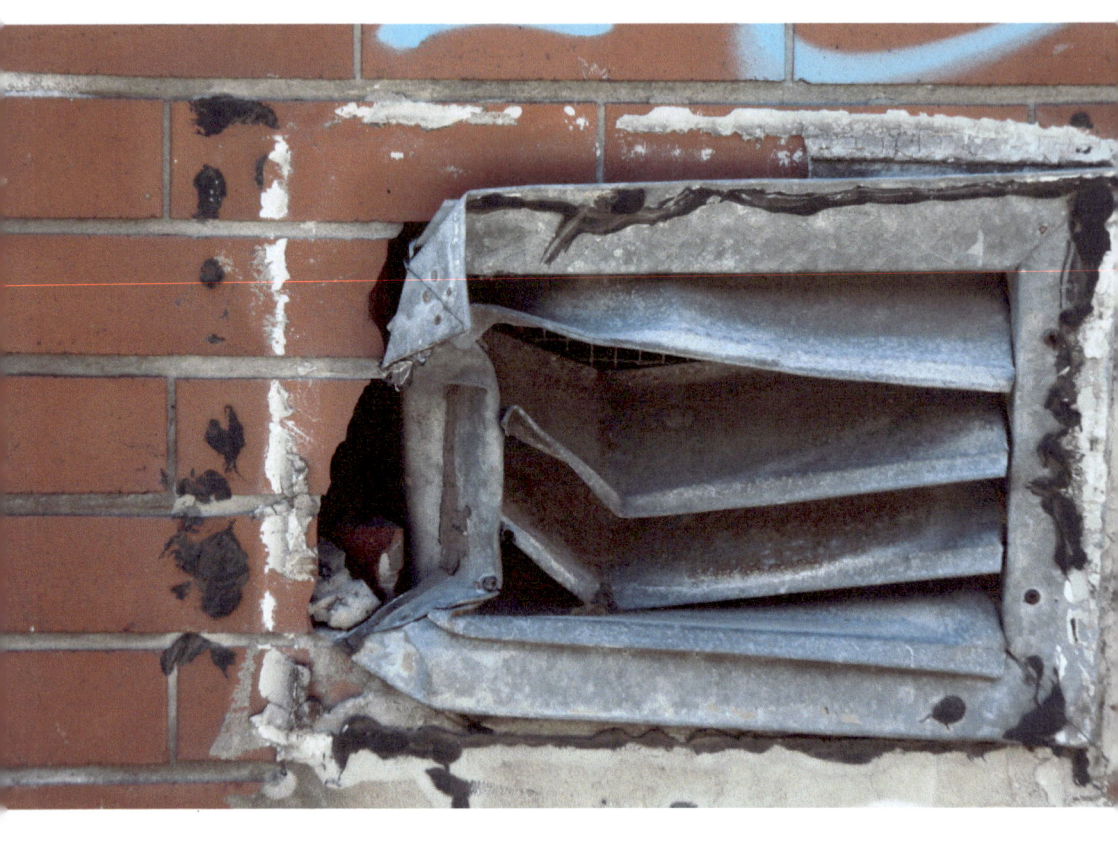

Amanda wanted a miracle. But she didn't seem to be making much progress. First she got a pumpkin, then pumpkin seeds, then a pumpkin garden, and then a pile of pumpkins, and then a porcelain pumpkin that she pulled out of thin air. But she didn't really *want* pumpkins. She wanted a miracle. A *specific* miracle.

She had finally gotten the courage to visit her grandfather (who seemed to be good with miracles). On his porch, she had been able to pull that nice porcelain pumpkin out of the air. She had also pulled a small green pumpkin out of the air. And three seeds. But she *still* hadn't gotten the miracle she wanted.

When Amanda got home, she tried to pull something else out of the air like she had done at her grandfather's. She tried for quite a while without success. At her grandfather's, Amanda had been surprised that she could do such a thing and that it had been so easy. But at home she got nothing.

Finally, Amanda decided to try with her eyes closed. She reached out and this time there *was* something. It was cold, soft and squishy, like the mushy inside of a pumpkin. Ick! She didn't want *that!* She wanted a miracle! She pulled her hands back and didn't try to get anything else out of the air.

Her best hope seemed to be the three seeds she had gotten from her grandfather.

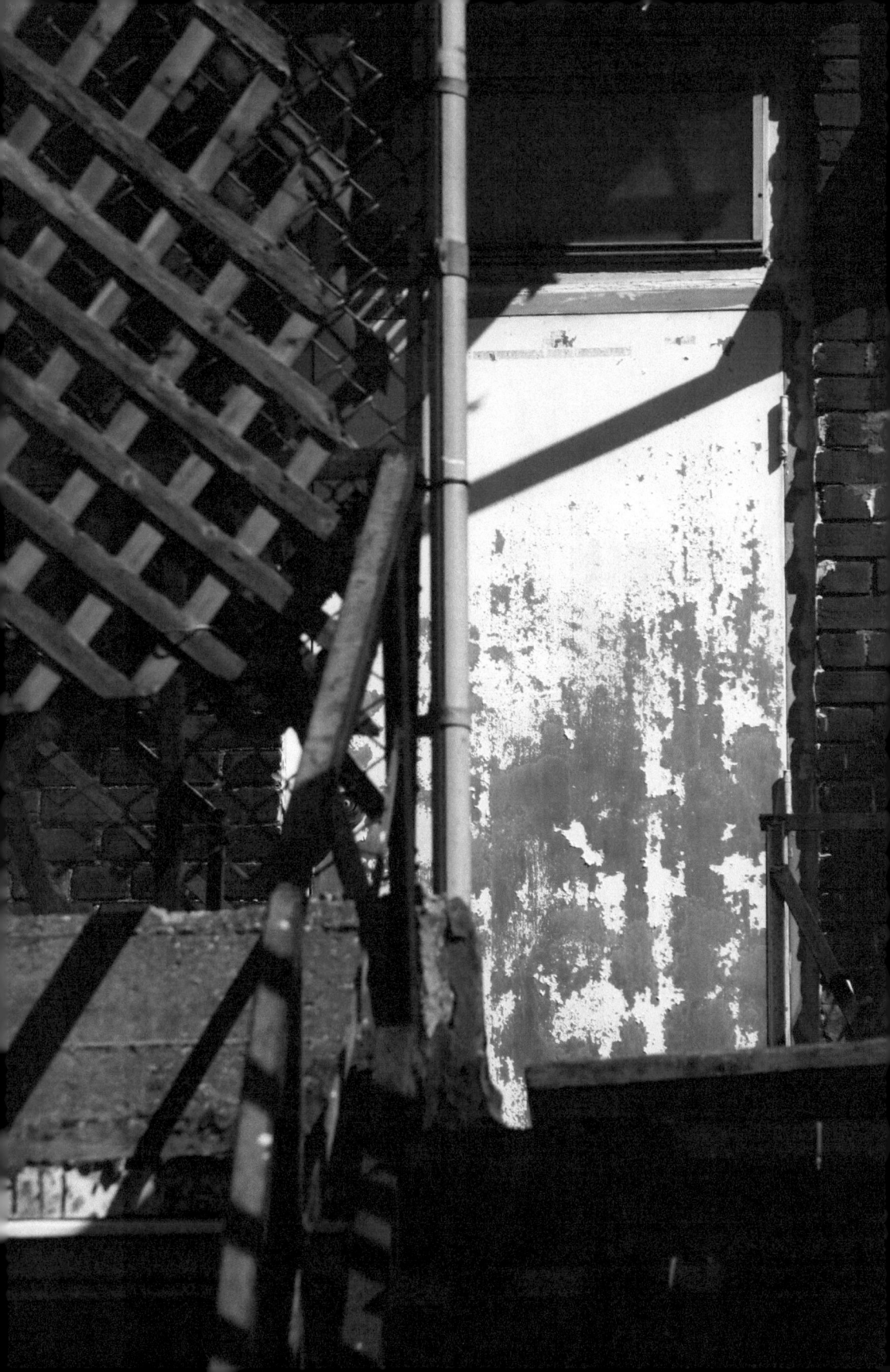

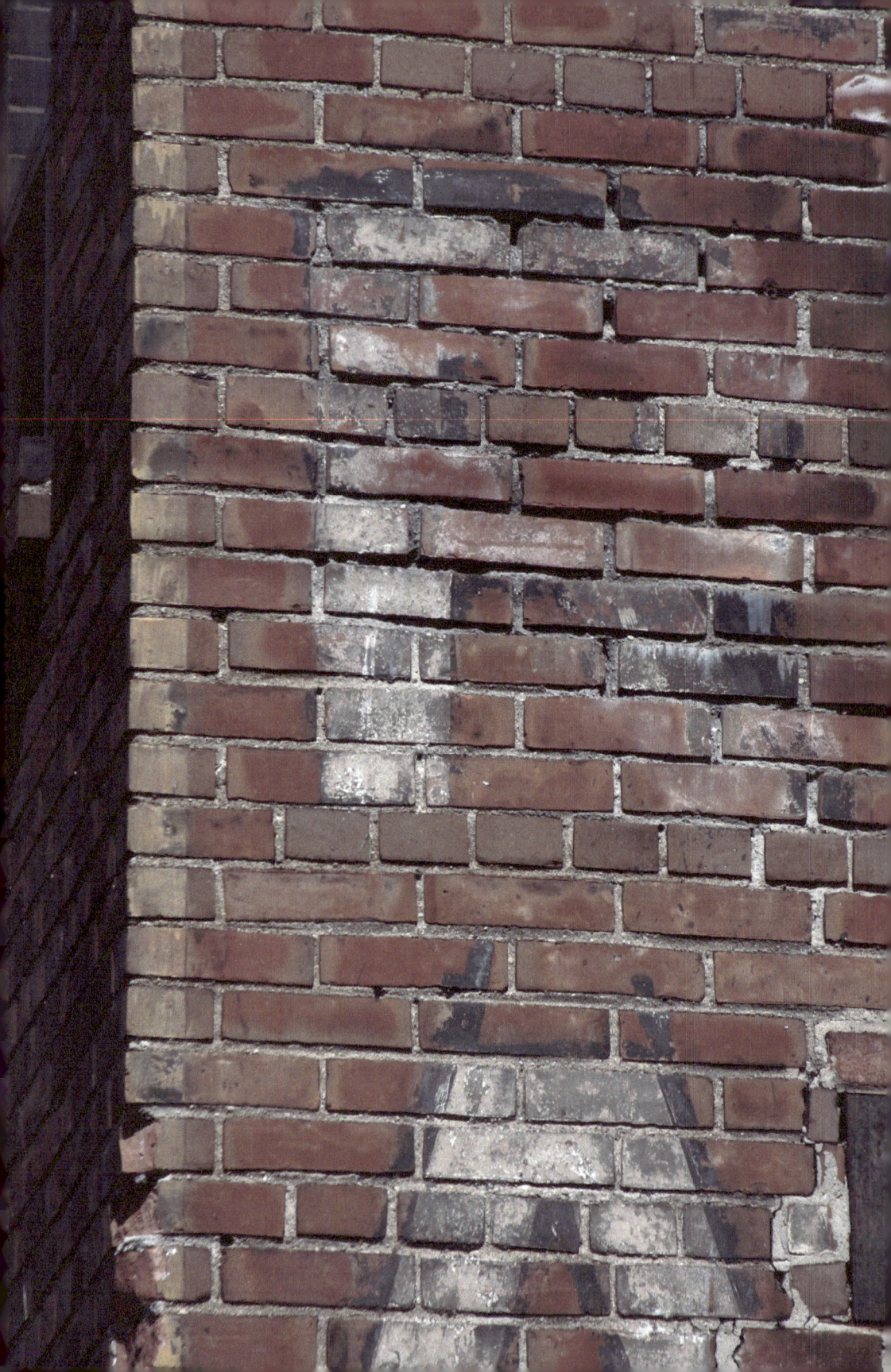

All winter the ground was frozen, and Amanda waited for spring so she could plant the seeds. She danced. She sang. She twirled. She smiled. Once in a while, she shrieked – mostly at her brother. She hated waiting. But eventually the snow melted and the ground thawed and – finally – it looked like it might be time to plant the seeds.

That night her grandmother called.

"Amanda dear," she said, "I've been doing research on those seeds of yours. For best results, you need to plant them in the next seven days. You'll have to water them every day – but not too much – and guard them against pests. And – this is the most important – do *not* plant them next to any pumpkins or watermelons. They don't get along well with pumpkins and watermelons."

Amanda said she would do her best. "Sometime in the next seven days," said her grandmother. "If I were you, I'd plant them tonight. You never know what will happen tomorrow. Good luck, Amanda." Then she hung up.

On impulse Amanda closed her eyes and stuck out her hands to see if she could pull another pumpkin from the air. When she opened her eyes she found she was holding a small porcelain snail. She tried again and got a porcelain slug. After that, she couldn't get anything else. She put the snail and slug on a shelf with her porcelain pumpkin.

Amanda wondered what kind of plants didn't get along with pumpkins or watermelons. She didn't know. But she *did* know she didn't want to plant any seeds that night in the dark.

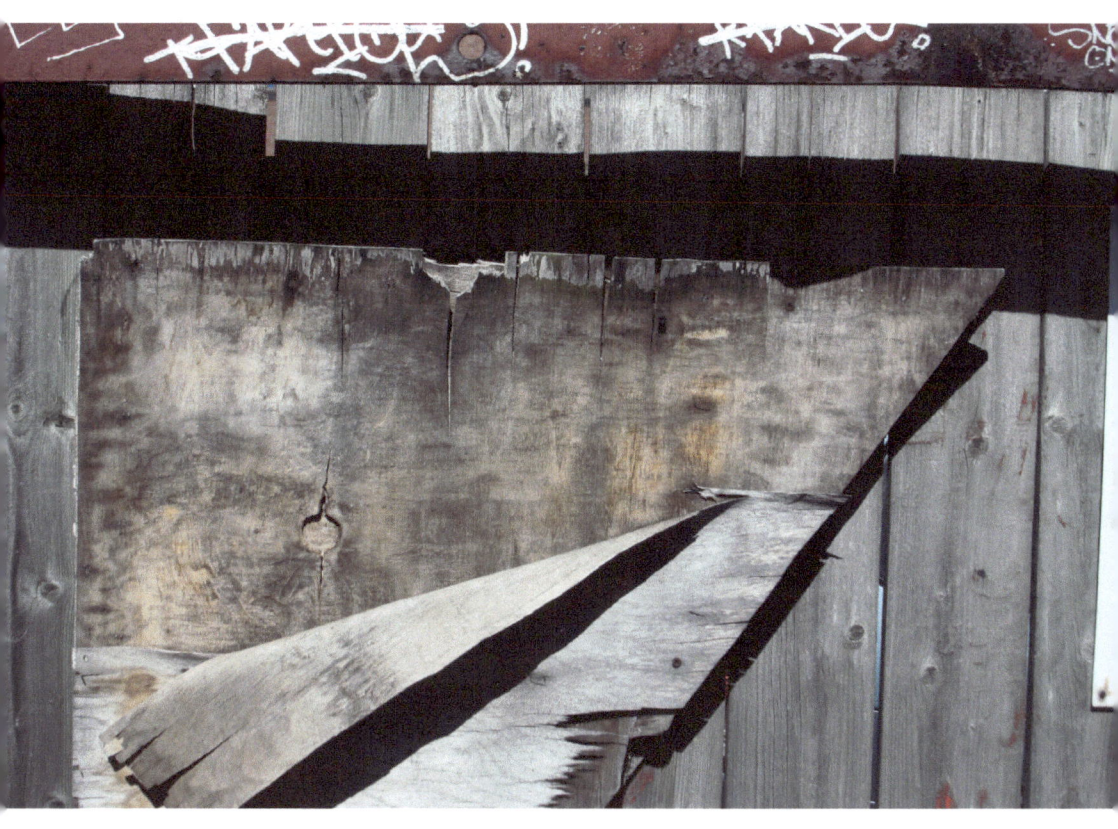

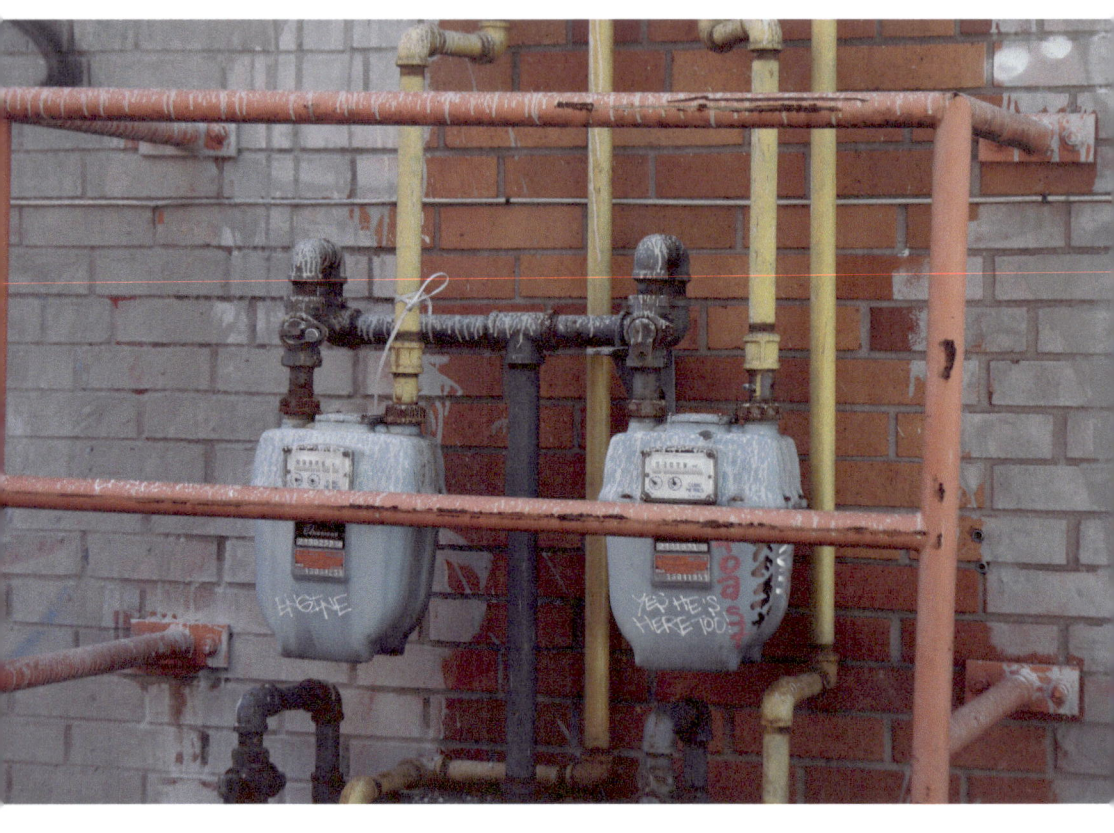

The next morning, just when Amanda was ready to plant the seeds, her mom called. "Amanda," she said, "I need your help packing."

"Packing?"

"Yes. We're going to your grandfather's house."

"I need to plant some seeds."

"There's no time. We have to get an early start. You can plant them when you get back."

Amanda couldn't believe it. "When will *that* be?" she asked.

"We're going to stay a week."

"A week! I can't be gone a week! I have to plant some seeds. And water them."

"Here's your suitcase dear. Pick out some clothes you like. And don't forget your toothbrush."

Amanda grabbed the suitcase, raced to her room, shoved some clothes and her toothbrush and stuffed bear into it and closed it fast. Then she raced to her garden.

"Amanda," her mom called after her. "There's no time. We have to leave. Your grandfather's on a very tight schedule. We'll get breakfast on the road. Your brother's already in the car."

Amanda hurriedly turned a shovelful of dirt upside down. It fell off the shovel in a thick clump. The soil wasn't really ready for seeds.

"Amanda," her mom called. "Get in the car. No more delays!"

Amanda used her thumb to push a small hole in the ground, put one of the seeds in it, and covered it with dirt. She didn't have time to plant the other two seeds. One would have to do. For now.

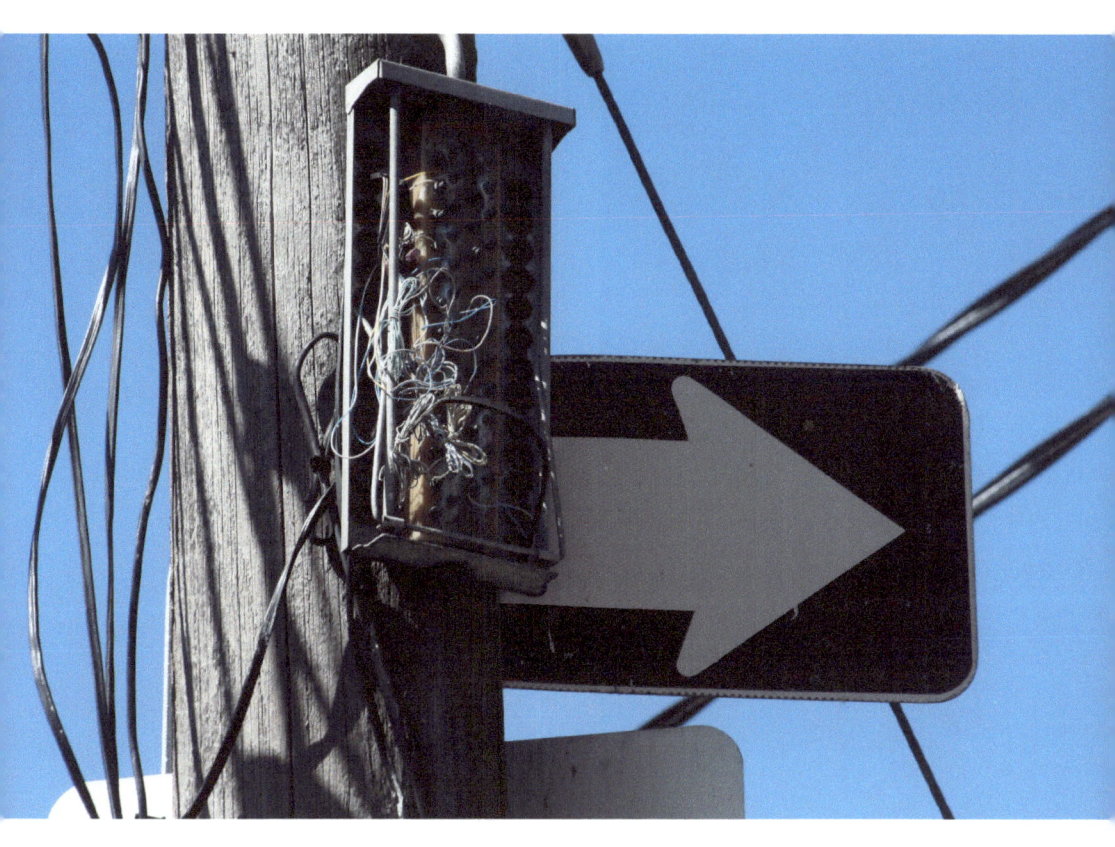

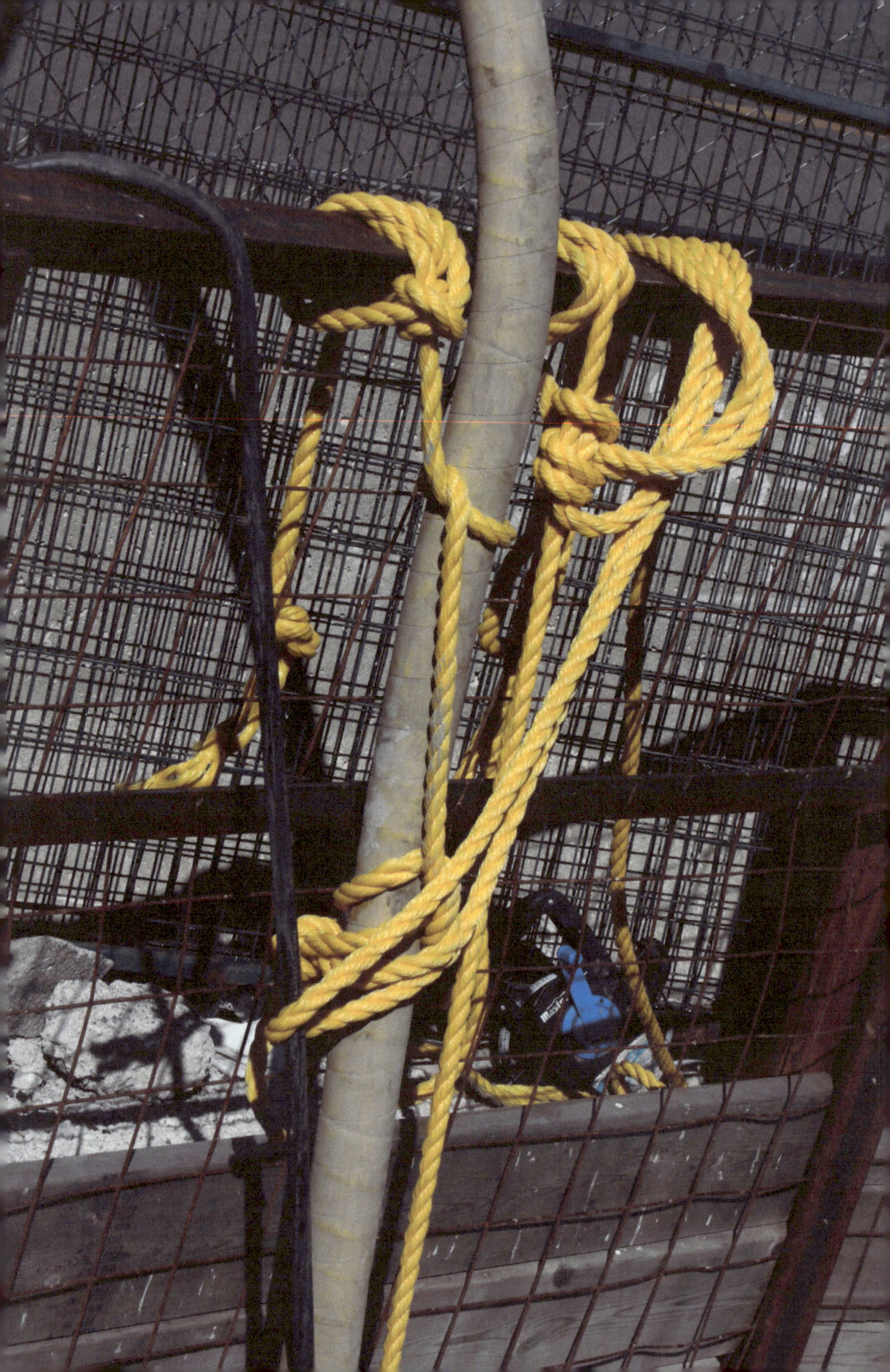

For the first part of the trip Amanda stared out the car window without talking, thinking about the seed she had just planted and the two seeds still in her pocket. She wondered why they had to go to her grandfather's *now*.

As they traveled, her mom told them they were going to take care of her grandfather's house while he was away on a trip. They'd only see him briefly when they arrived and briefly when he got back.

On the journey, Amanda played games with her brother. She took a nap. She sang songs. She even did some homework. The drive took forever. They had breakfast along the way, then lunch, then dinner. At last, late at night, they finally got to her grandfather's. Amanda couldn't understand why they hadn't taken the Number Six bus.

When they arrived, the porch light was on. A note was tacked to the door.

> Sorry I had to leave before you got here. I didn't want to be late. Thanks for taking care of my place. I'll see you when I get back. Love, Grandpa.

On the porch, Amanda stuck out her hands and pulled a porcelain mouse out of thin air. She put it in her pocket before anyone could notice and ask questions. Then she stepped inside the house.

Amanda had never been inside her grandfather's house before. It was enormous. And she had a whole week to explore. At any other time she would have been thrilled. But this was the week she was supposed to be planting three seeds.

Amanda was worried and didn't know what to do. She left the light on in her room that night while she slept.

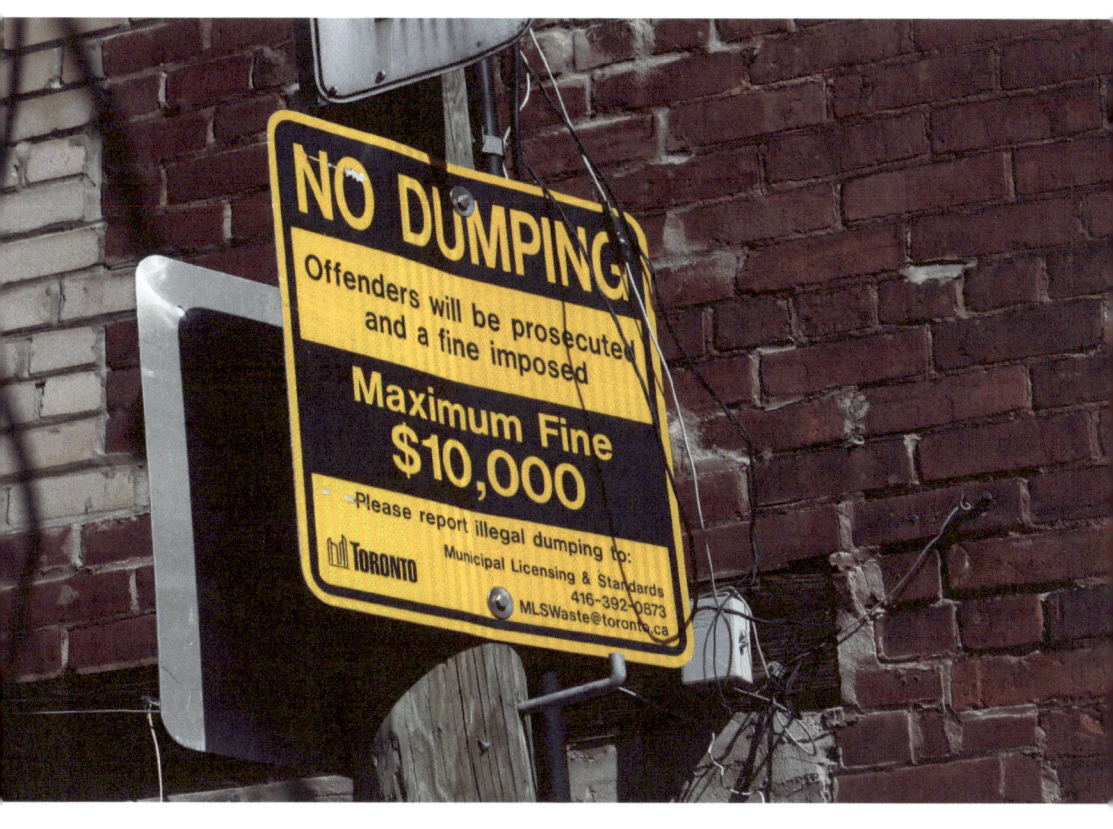

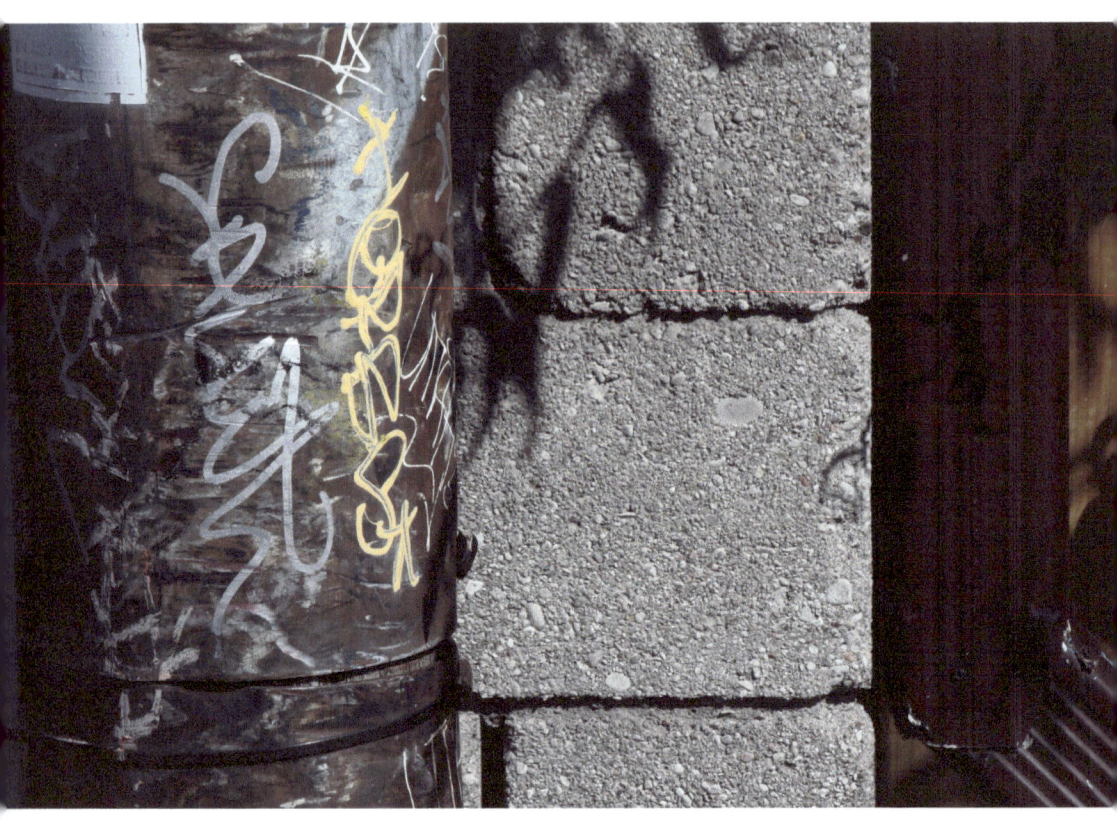

The next morning Amanda got her chores for the week. One of the chores was to water and weed her grandfather's garden. Amanda went out to inspect it.

The garden was freshly tilled. Empty seed packs marked each row. One row was for herbs. One row was for tomatoes, peppers and peas. One was for squash, beans and rutabagas. One whole section was for corn. Amanda was surprised to see that a row was reserved for pumpkins. She didn't think her grandfather *liked* pumpkins. But she was not surprised to find that *most* of the garden was for watermelons. Rows and rows and rows of them.

Amanda found one small patch towards the back of the enormous garden that was still empty. It was a little close to the pumpkins and fairly close to the watermelons. But she decided to plant the second seed there anyway. She had only six more days to plant the last two seeds, and it was likely she'd be at her grandfather's the whole time. Amanda got the soil ready, planted the seed and watered it.

Then she remembered she should be watering the seed she had planted at home. Now what?

She didn't know.

Each day, Amanda took care of her grandfather's garden, watering, weeding and watching for pests in the morning. In the afternoon, she played in the yard with her brother. In the evening, she wandered the house, looking at her grandfather's many books. Every now and then she went to the porch and pulled something out of the air. After a few days she had a family of mice, a rabbit, a mole, and a spider, all made out of fine porcelain.

Twice when she reached for some nice, fine porcelain she touched something cold, squishy and icky instead. She withdrew her hands quickly when that happened.

On the third day, her grandfather called. "Amanda," he asked, "Have you planted those seeds yet?"

"Two of them," she said.

"That's good. Who did you get to water them?"

Amanda gulped. She hadn't gotten *anyone* to water the seed planted at *her* house. She was just about to admit that when her grandfather cut in. "Oh!" he said. "I'm late. Sorry. I have to go. Tell everyone I love them and thanks for taking care of my house and garden. Bye!" He hung up.

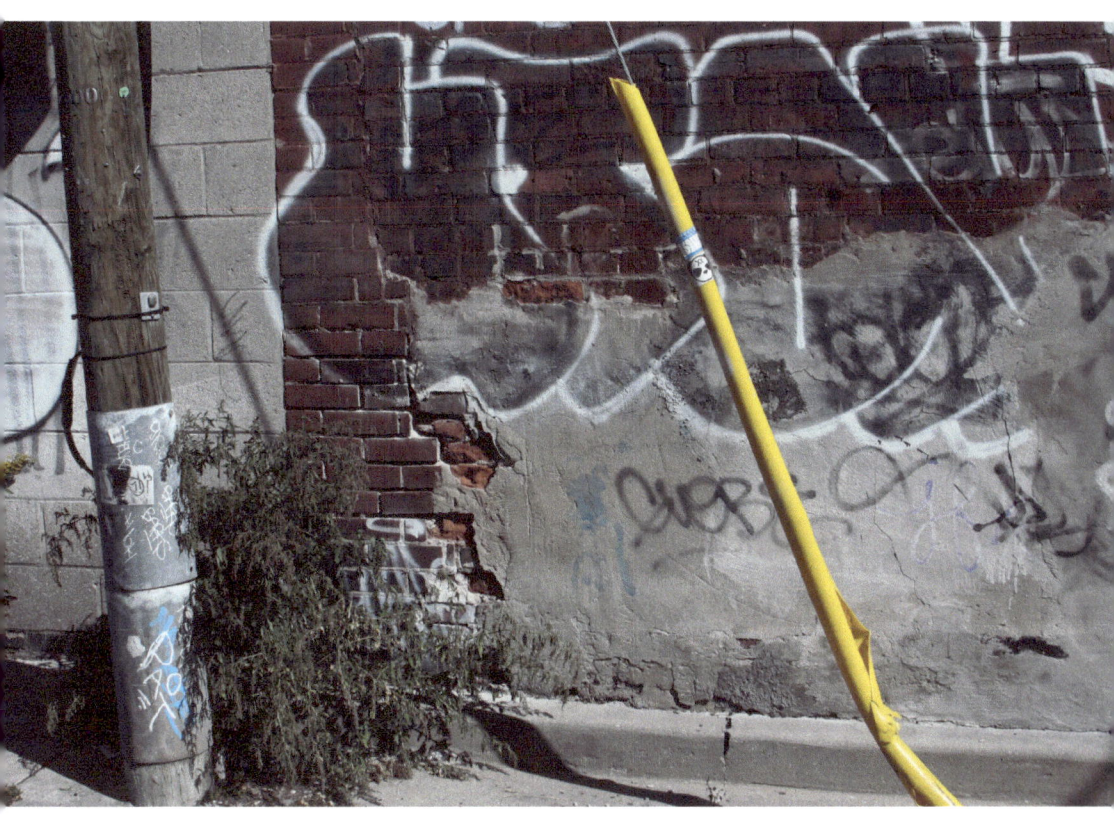

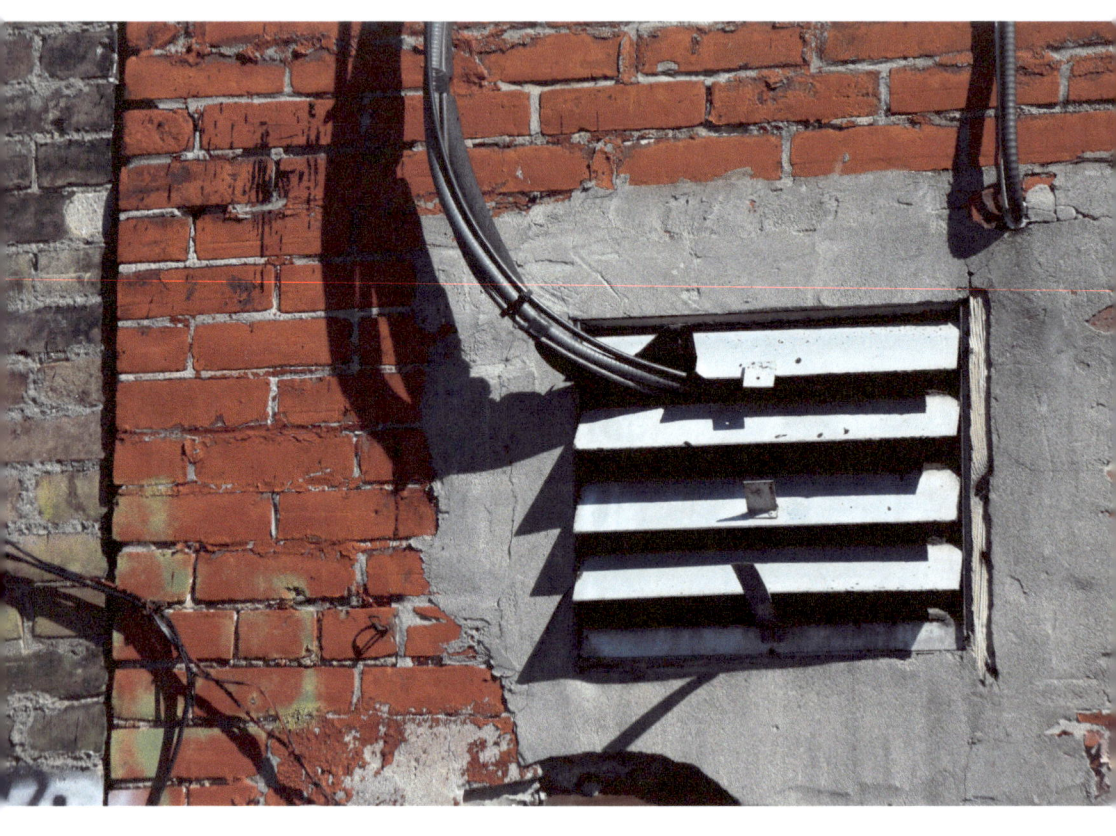

Amanda relayed the message. "Grandpa says thanks for taking care of his house and garden," she said. "And he loves us." Then she went out to the garden. The seed she had planted had already sprouted and grown a foot. It was growing much faster than her pumpkin plants – or anything else she had seen.

Amanda decided she *had* to get water to the seed in her garden at home. She called her grandmother and asked her to water it until she got back. Then Amanda spent the next three days gardening and reading and playing with her brother and – when no one was looking – pulling more porcelain out of the air. She pulled a porcelain dog, cat, porcupine, horse and weasel out of the air. She found she had as much luck inside the house as she had on the porch. But she had the most luck standing in the garden next to her new plant.

In the garden, the porcelain she pulled out of the air was starting to be exceptionally beautiful. But in the garden she also accidentally touched the cold, squishy, icky stuff the most. She tried to avoid the cold glop, but sometimes it got in the way. After a few attempts where all she could feel was the squishy stuff, she would quit for a few hours, or try someplace in the house instead.

On the fifth day at her grandfather's, all the watermelon plants sprouted. Amanda walked down the long rows of plants, admiring them until she got to her own patch at the back of the garden. There she was shocked to see her beautiful plant was drooping. The day before it had been vibrant and lush. But now it looked like it was gasping for air, barely alive. She watered it, but that didn't help.

Amanda called her grandmother at noon. "Amanda, dear," said her grandmother. "I have some bad news. The new plant in your garden didn't make it. By the time I got to your house, it had died from lack of water. I've watered it every day since you called, but I don't think it'll come back."

Amanda thanked her grandmother, then set down the phone in silence. She blinked back a tear. She had one dead plant at her house, one dying plant at her grandfather's, and a seed that had to be planted in a day or two or it would be too late. Things weren't going very well. She hoped her grandfather would get home soon.

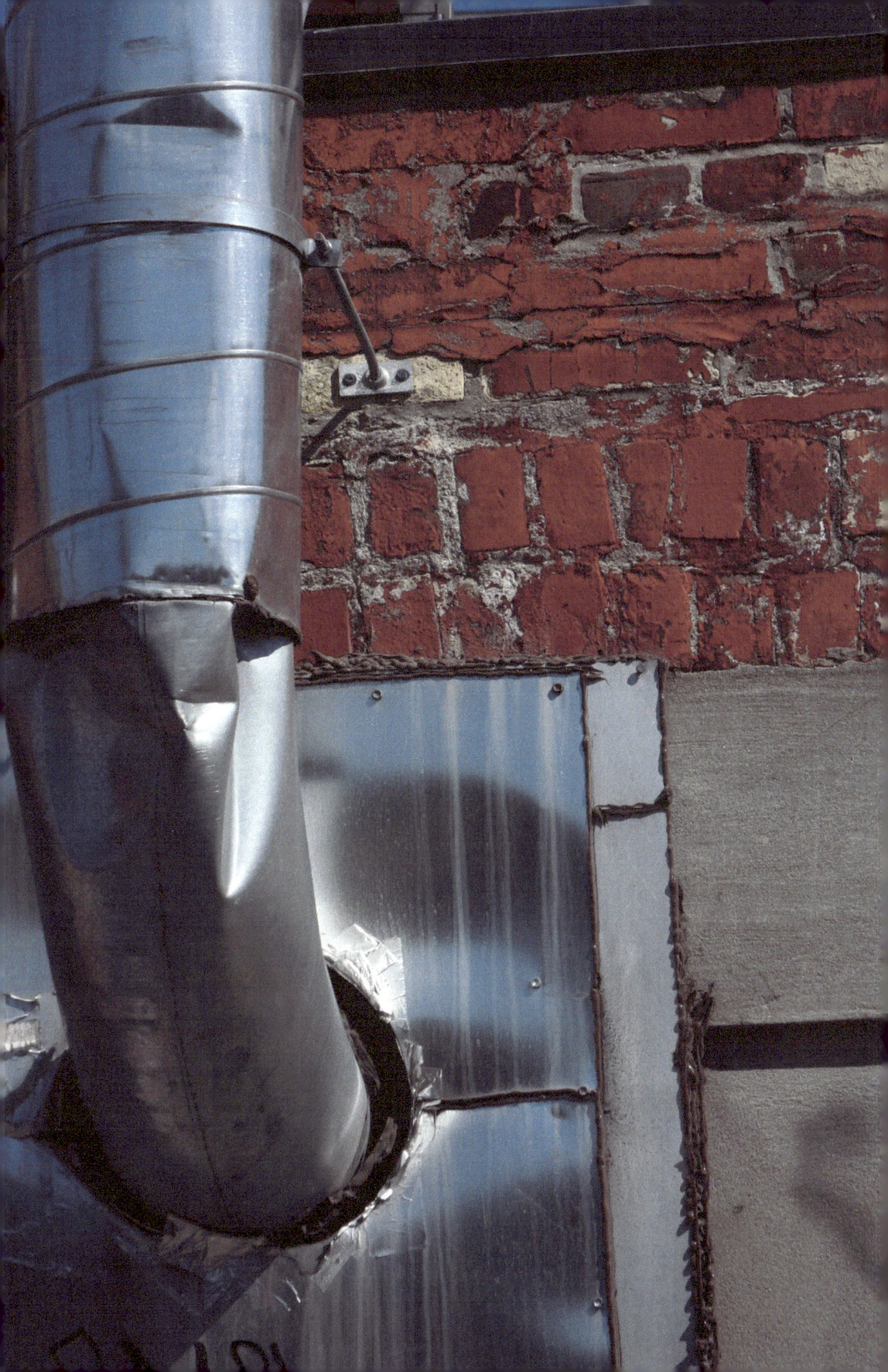

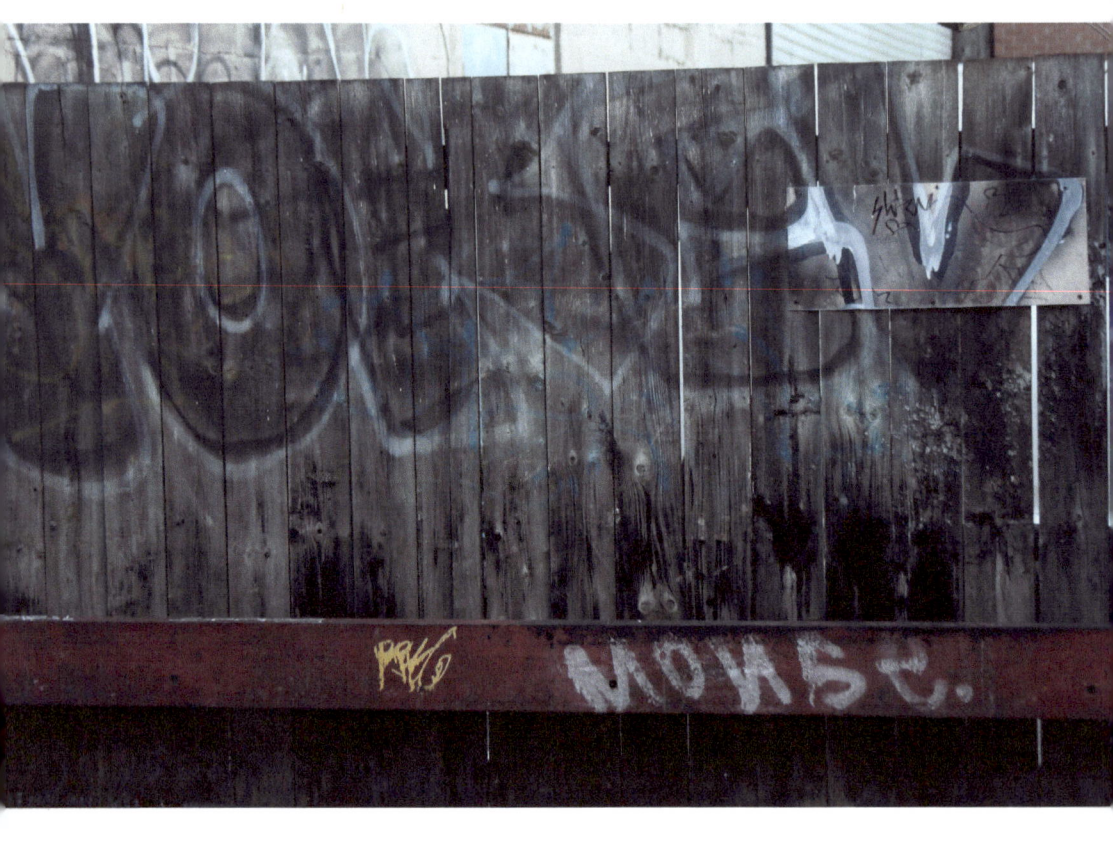

That afternoon her grandfather called. "Something doesn't feel right," he said. "Tell me about the seeds you planted."

Amanda gulped. Then she blurted it out. "I planted one seed at home just before we left. But grandma says it died because it wasn't watered."

"Hmm," said her grandfather. "I've made that mistake."

"Then I planted one here."

"At *my* house?" said her grandfather. "Where?"

"At the back of the garden. In a patch that wasn't planted yet."

Her grandfather laughed. "You don't have to tell me how *that* seed is doing. It's *way* too close to the pumpkins and watermelons. I bet it's already sagging."

"Yes," said Amanda. "It doesn't look good."

"Well, that's too bad, but don't worry about it. I've tried *lots* of those seeds there with no success. What about the third seed?"

"It's in my pocket," Amanda said.

Her grandfather smiled broadly and he almost laughed again. "Amanda dear, you do *not* want to keep it in your pocket," he said. "If it starts to grow there, you will be in *big* trouble." He paused. "I've seen you pull porcelain out of the air at my house. Do you think you can put the seed into the air for safe keeping and then pull it back out when you need it?"

"I *think* so," said Amanda. She had never tried such a thing, but it sounded possible. At least it sounded as possible as pulling porcelain from the air.

"Practice quite a bit while you're at my house," said her grandfather. "But don't keep the seed in your pocket any more, because it needs to take root within a day or so. You've got to get it in the ground soon. At *your* house. So *you* can water it. It won't do you much good if it's at my house and I'm the one doing all the watering. It also won't do you much good if your grandmother is doing all the watering. *You* need to do the watering if it's going to help you. I didn't realize the seeds weren't planted when I asked your mom to stay at my house for a week." He paused again, then said, "Let me talk to your mother."

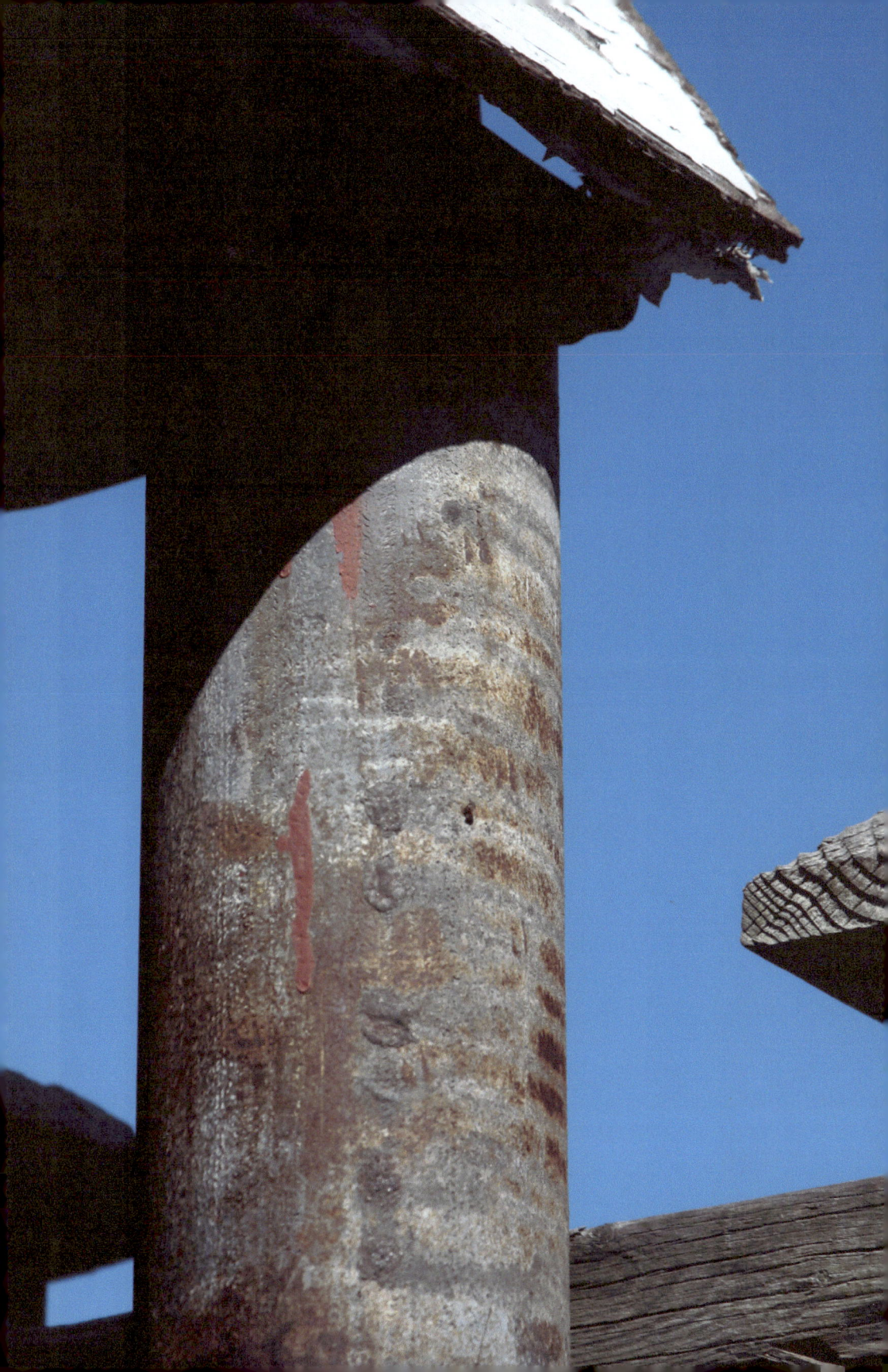

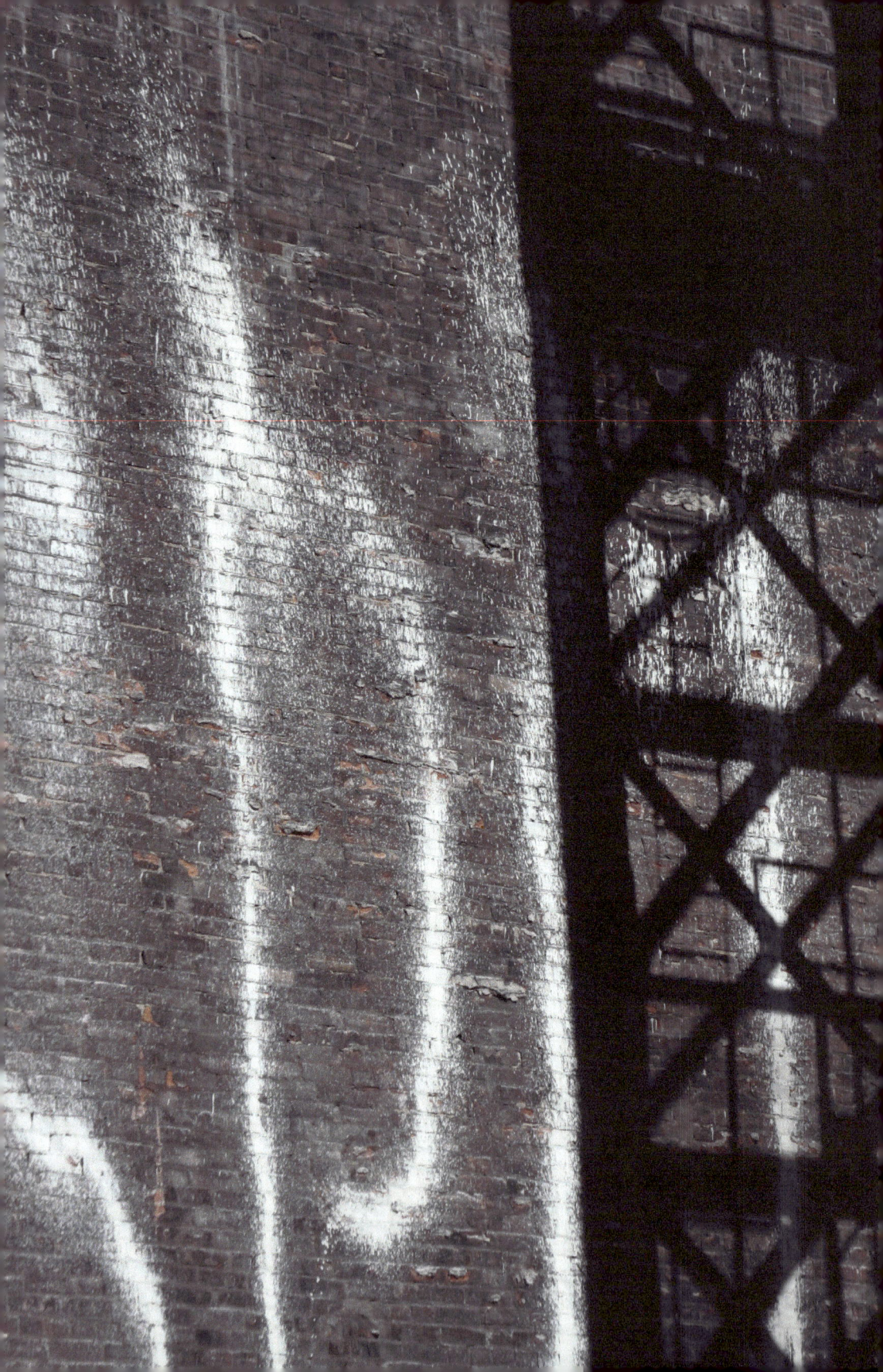

A minute later, Amanda's mom hung up the phone and announced they would be leaving early the next morning. They would miss seeing their grandfather, who wouldn't return until that night. Amanda's mom didn't say why they were leaving early. "But," Amanda thought hopefully, "maybe I'll get home in time to plant the last seed."

For the rest of the day Amanda practiced putting the seed into the air and taking it back out. Sometimes when she tried to put it into the air her hands got entangled in the cold, icky mush. When that happened, she pulled her hands back until she found someplace drier. Sometimes when she reached to retrieve the seed, she pulled out a nice porcelain seed instead. But by the end of the day she had gotten enough practice so she was fairly confident she could keep the seed in the air and pull it out when she needed it, even at home.

That night Amanda packed all her porcelain treasures and her clothes so she would be ready to leave the next day. She left a beautiful porcelain mouse as a gift for her grandfather.

The drive home was just as long as the trip over had been. It took all day. When they finally arrived, Amanda raced to her garden. She could see where her grandmother had watered, but her new plant looked quite dead. Amanda carefully prepared the soil near it. She didn't want the last seed to die, too. When the soil was ready, she planted the last seed and stepped back.

Her mom called. "Phone, Amanda."

"I'm busy," she yelled.

"It's your grandfather."

Amanda raced to the phone.

"Did you plant the last seed?" he asked.

"I just finished," Amanda said.

"Good," he said. "I think that will be in time. Thank you for the nice mouse."

Amanda hesitated. But she *had* to ask.

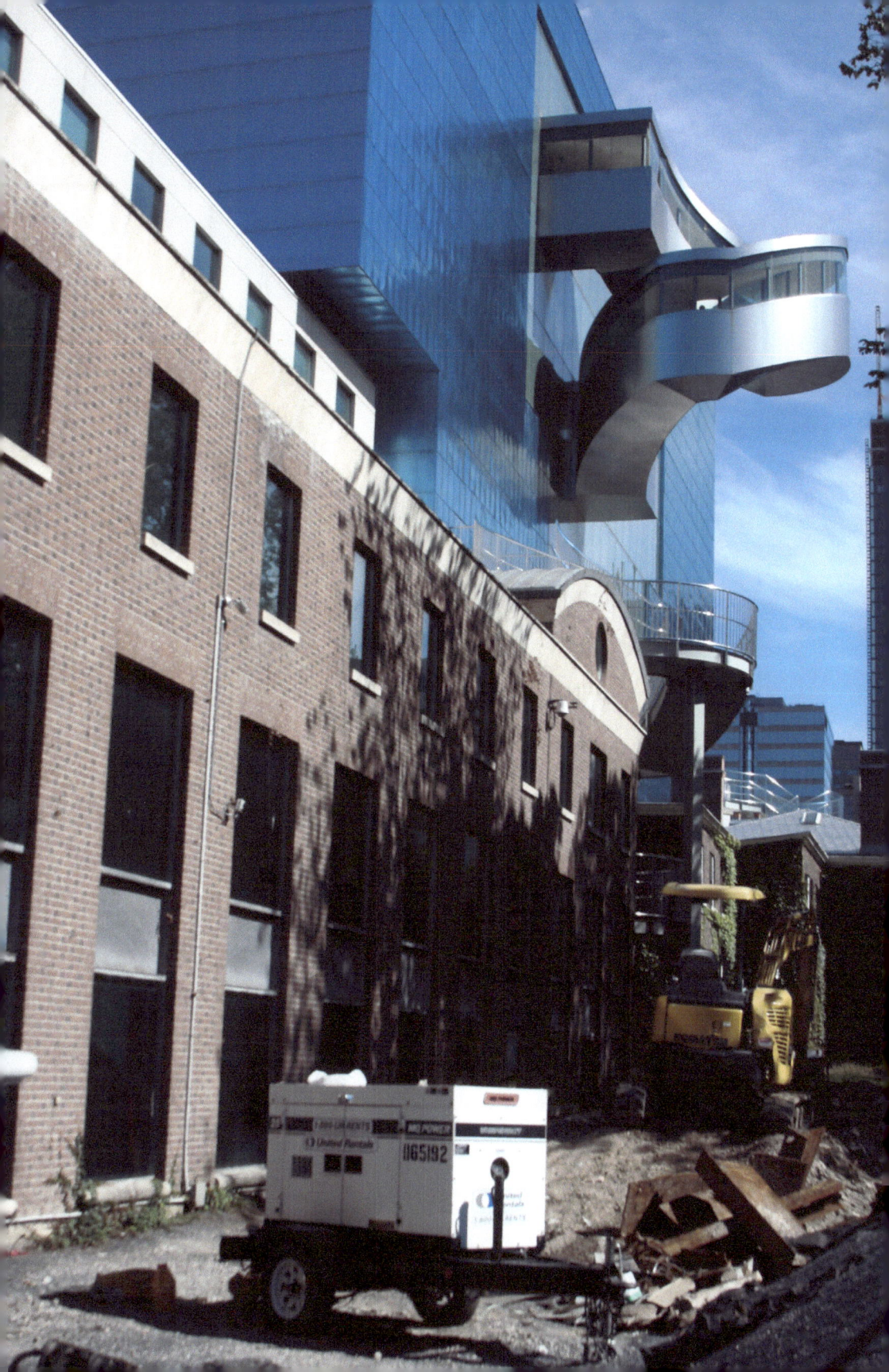

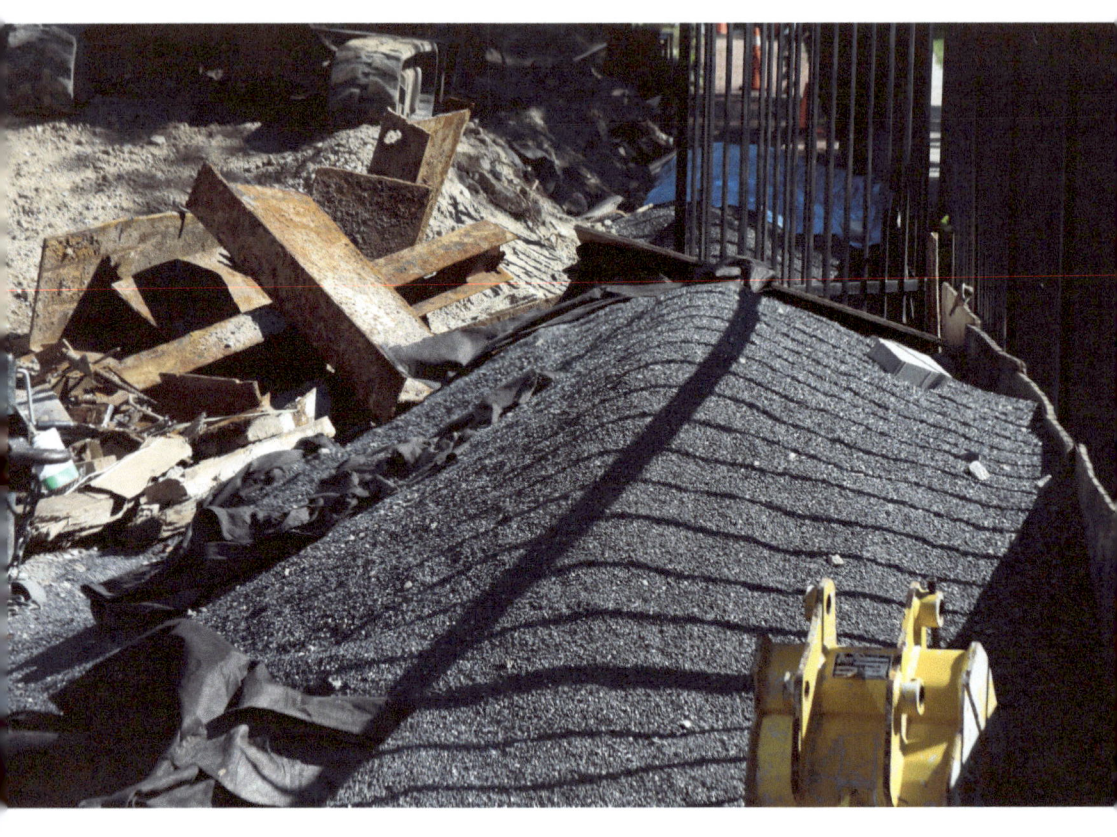

"Grandpa," she said. "Sometimes I reach for a nice porcelain mouse or something and I touch something cold, icky and mushy instead."

"At *my* house?" her grandfather asked. "At *my* house? You touched something cold, icky and squishy at *my* house? Amanda, you're getting quite good!"

Amanda didn't know what to make of his comment.

"What did you do with it?" he asked.

"I pulled my hands back so I wouldn't have to touch it," she said.

"Oh, Amanda," he said. "Don't do *that!* It's the miracle you've been hoping for! It's trying to find you – and much sooner than I thought it would. The next time you feel it, grab hold and don't let go. Pull it out of the air with all your might. It may not feel or look like much at first, but that's definitely the miracle you've been hoping for."

"Grandpa," Amanda said. "That *can't* be my miracle. It feels icky, like a glop of pumpkin seeds inside a cold pumpkin."

"Well," he said, "A bunch of watermelon seeds probably *would* feel *much* nicer. I imagine it feels like pumpkin seeds because you learned so much from your grandmother. But that's your miracle, alright. It'll feel different after you pull it out of the air and let it grow a bit."

Amanda was too surprised to say anything more.

"I'm glad you're so close to getting what you want, Amanda," said her grandfather. "But I really have to go. Thanks again for the mouse. I put it by your plant in the garden. It looks like the mouse might help your plant recover, even though it's so close to all those watermelons."

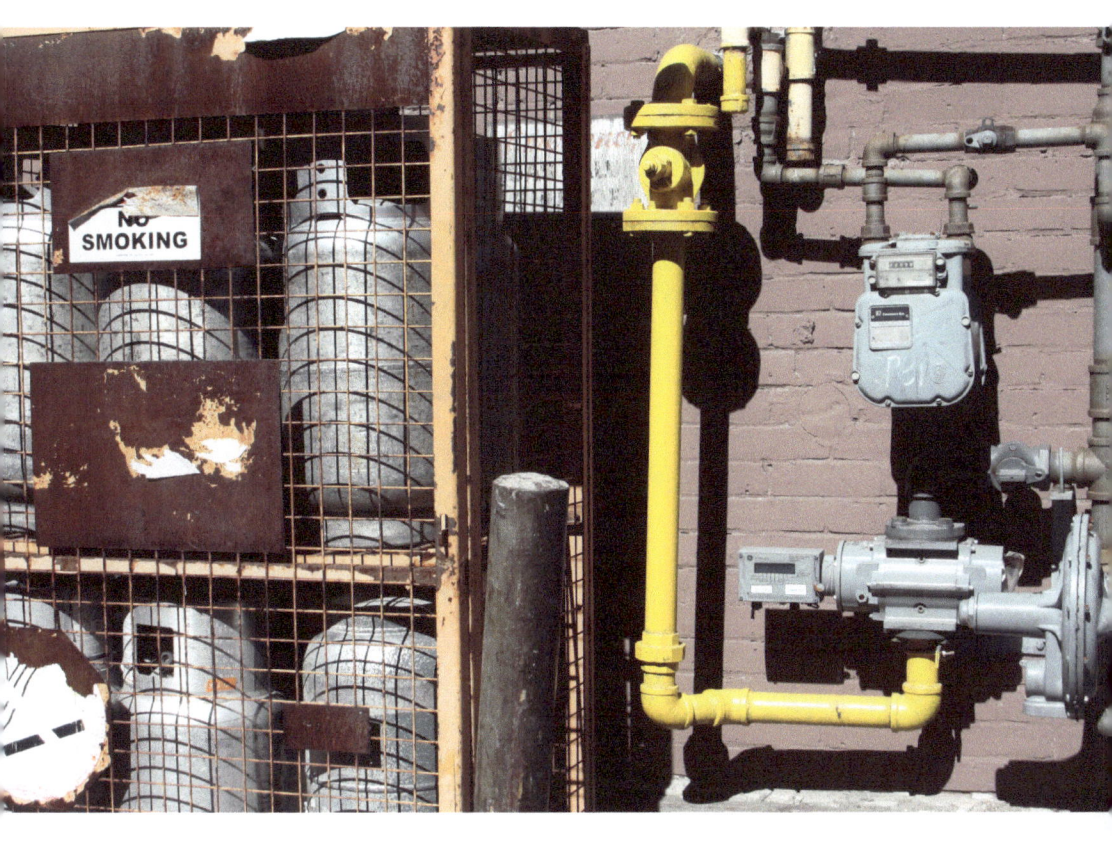

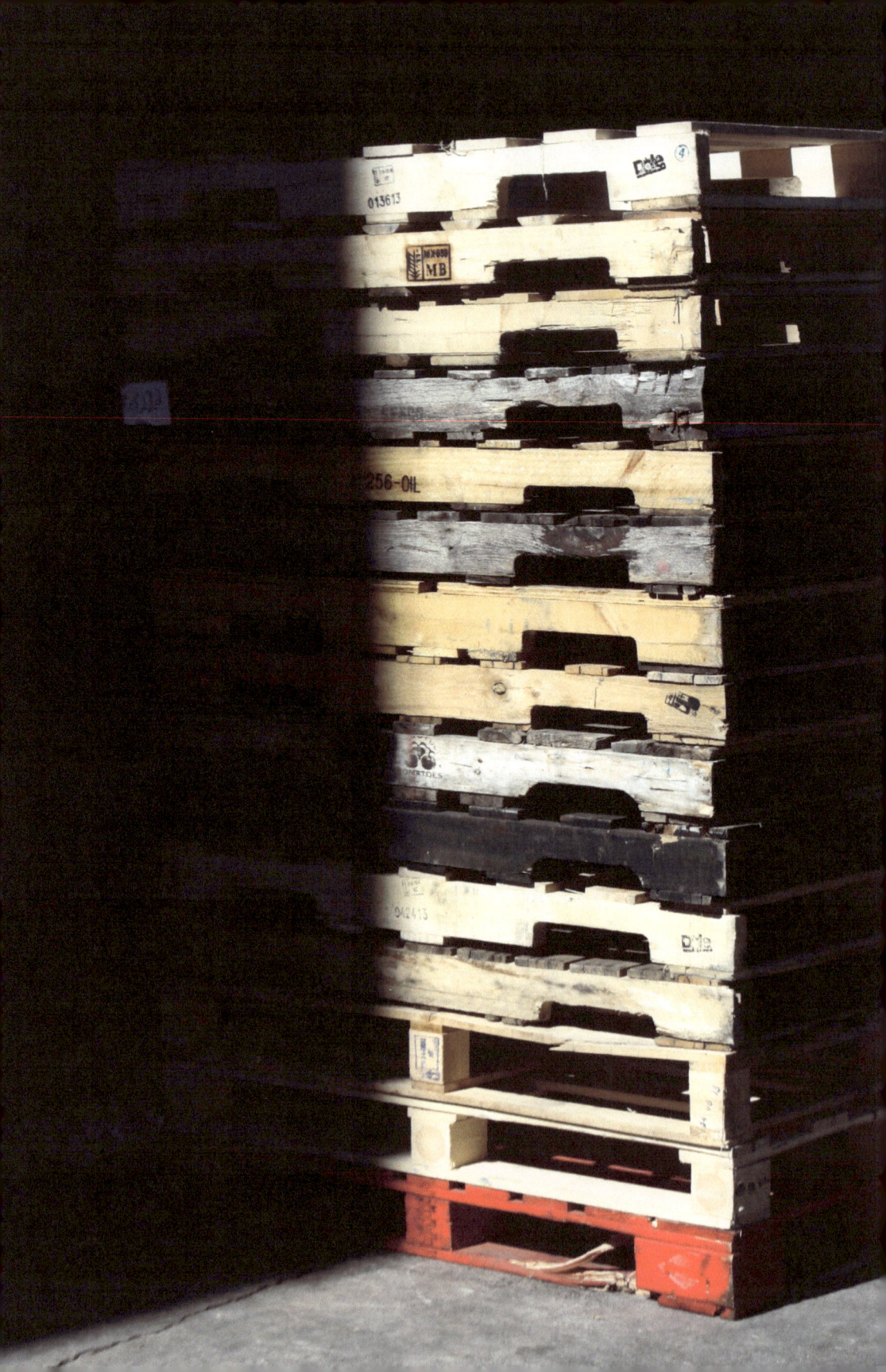

"What?" said Amanda.

"Everybody's good at something," said her grandfather. "Usually it's for a reason. At the moment, porcelain seems to be your thing. If I were you, I'd put a few porcelain creatures in your garden at home, just to see what happens. But I really *have* to go. Love you." Then the phone clicked and he was gone.

Amanda stood by the phone a few seconds, stunned at the news that the drooping plant at her grandfather's might recover. After a bit she shook herself, went to her room, scooped up all the porcelain figures in her suitcase and carried them to the garden. She put them near the dead plant and the spot where she had buried the third seed. Then she went back to the house and got ready for bed.

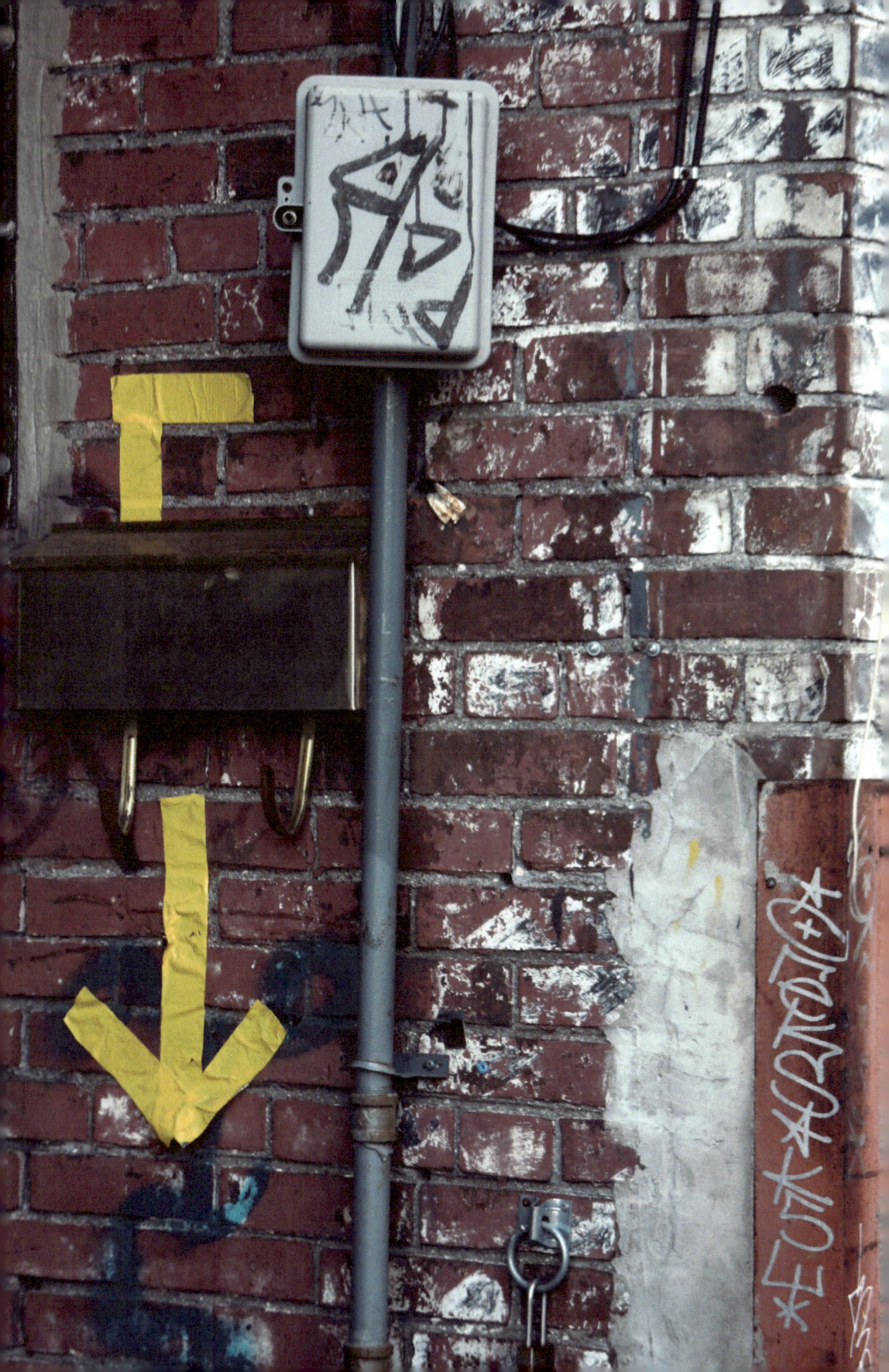

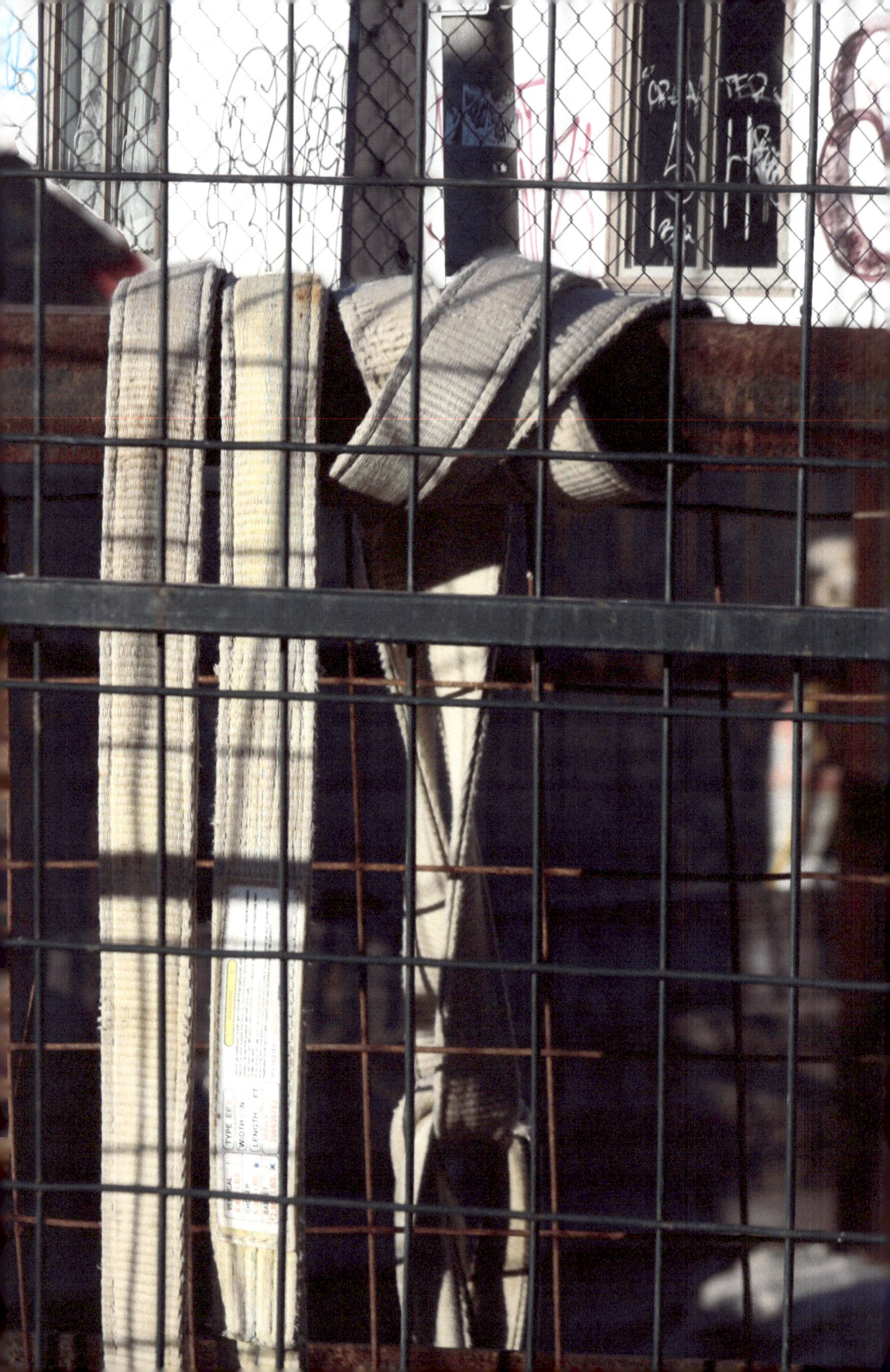

That night, while she was dreaming, the dead plant put out a new shoot. Later that night, the third seed sprouted. Then both plants started to grow. And grow. And grow.

Meanwhile, Amanda was dreaming that she was covered in cold, mushy pumpkin glop. But – at least in her dream – she was surprised to find it wasn't quite as icky as she had first supposed.

Reflection questions

When have you discovered that something you were avoiding was something that you actually wanted?

What kind of miracles are you hoping for today?

If you bumped into them when they were disguised, would you recognize them?

What kinds of disguises might they wear?

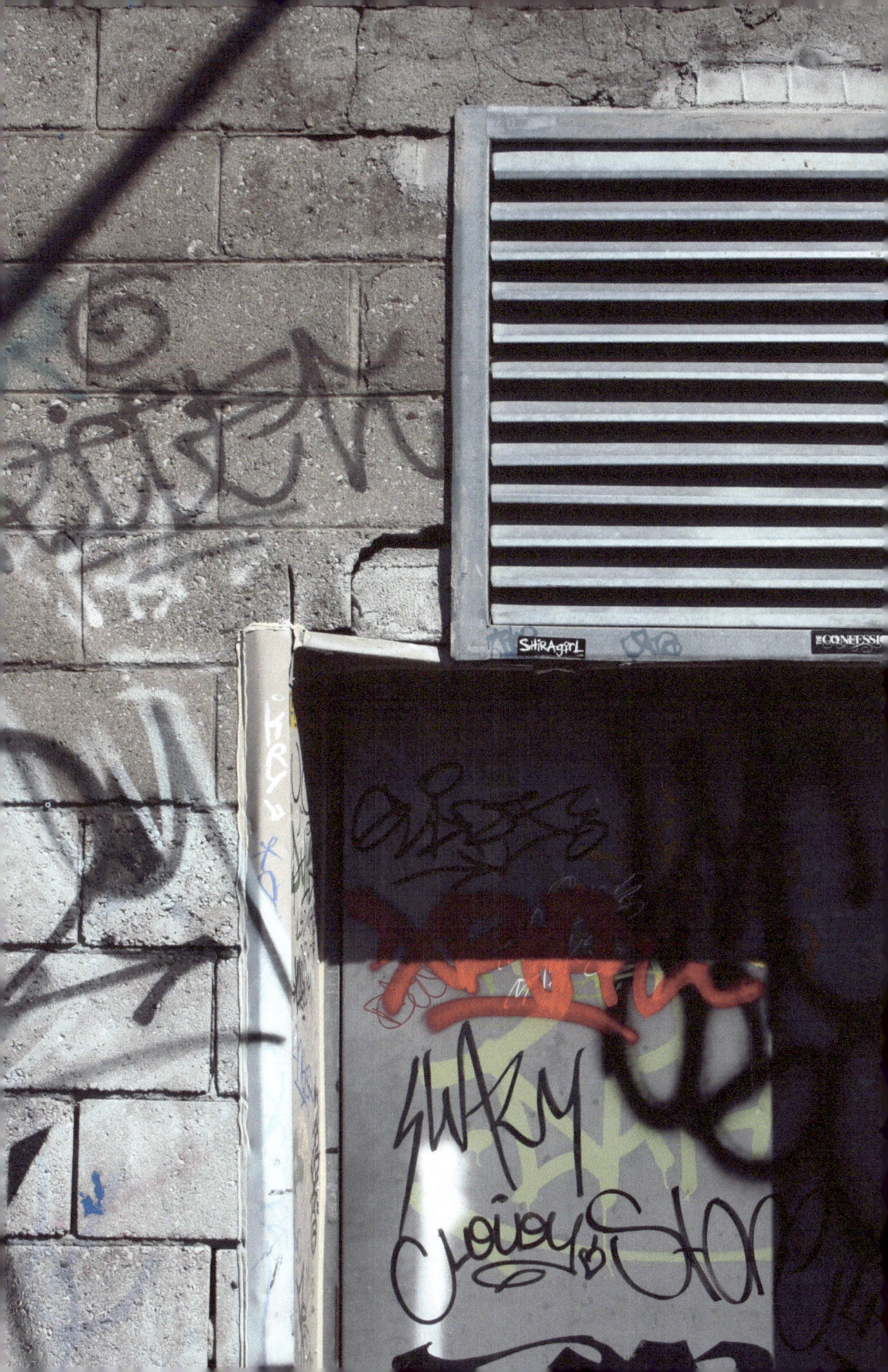

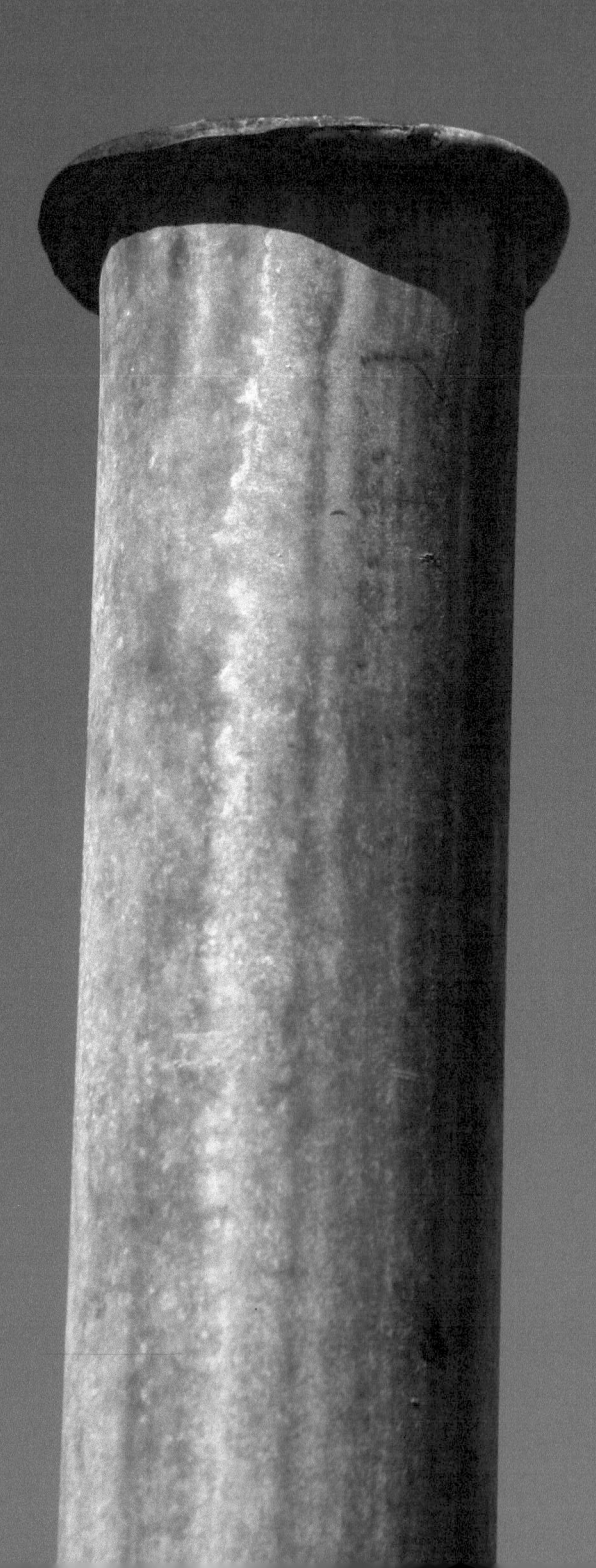

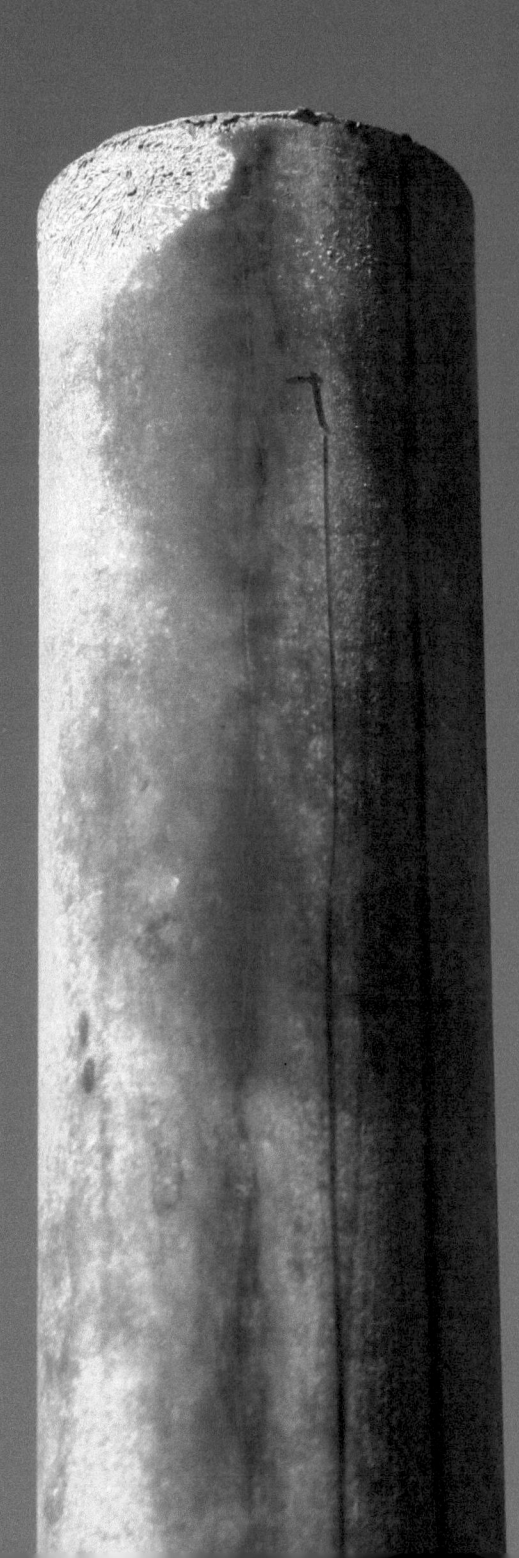

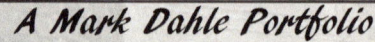

Amanda Gets A Neighbor

(#4 in the series Amanda Wanted A Miracle)

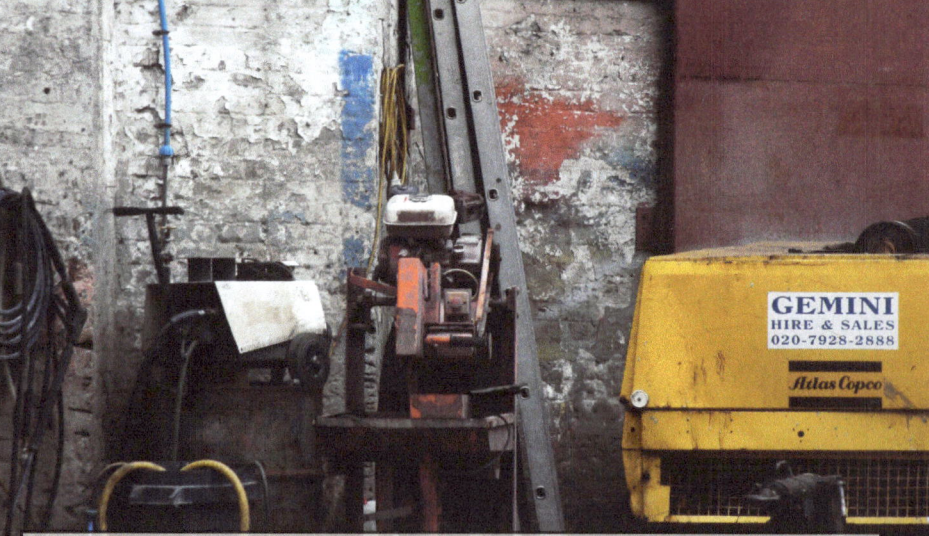

GEMINI
HIRE & SALES
020-7928-2888

Atlas Copco

This Mark Dahle Portfolio includes a colorful painting, twenty-four beautiful industrial photographs from London, and a story about a girl who wanted a miracle but got a neighbor instead.

His face was as red as a radish, and he was scowling and holding his big nose.

This Mark Dahle Portfolio includes a colorful painting, twenty-six beautiful photographs from Detroit, and a story about a carpenter who made fine furniture from scraps.

The carpenter came across the twig one day while scouring the countryside for debris. He had already found a sheet of plastic, a broken piece of plywood and several rusty, bent nails. Those he knew he could use. But the twig? He could not imagine a use for it. Nevertheless, it caught his attention as he walked along the edge of a forest. He absentmindedly picked it up.

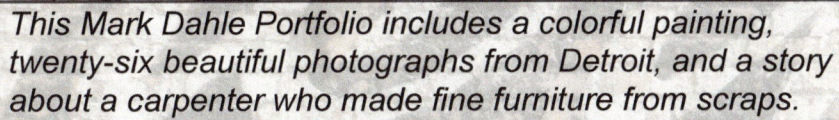

A Mark Dahle Portfolio

The Carpenter And The Twig

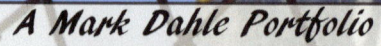

A Mark Dahle Portfolio

The Grasshopper And The Flea

Some Things Never Change

(Fables About Aesop #1)

This Mark Dahle Portfolio includes a colorful painting, twenty-six beautiful photographs of fences in Basel, Switzerland, and a story about Aesop having remarkable difficulties writing a story.

Aesop liked the morals at the end of his stories to stay put. But he had just written about a grasshopper and a flea, and the moral was hopping around.